Contents

Luther Reed

The Legacy of a Gentleman and a Churchman

Philip H. Pfatteicher

Lutheran University Press
Minneapolis, Minnesota

Luther Reed
The Legacy of a Gentleman and a Churchman
by Philip H. Pfatteicher

Published under the auspices of:
    Center for Church Music
    Concordia University Chicago
    River Forest, IL 60305-1402

ISBN: 978-1-942304-05-0

Lutheran University Press
PO Box 390759
Minneapolis, MN 55439
Manufactured in the United States of America

About the Center for Church Music

The Center for Church Music was established in 2010 on the campus of Concordia University Chicago.

Its purpose is to provide ongoing research and educational resources in Lutheran church music especially in the areas of congregational song and composition for the Church. It is intended to be of interest to pastors, musicians, and laity alike.

The Center maintains a continually expanding resource room which houses the Schalk American Lutheran Hymnal Collection, the manuscript collections of prominent Lutheran composers and hymn writers, and a broad array of reference works and resources in church music. To create a global awareness and facilitate online research efforts are underway to digitize the hymnal collection, the manuscript archives, and the hymn festival recordings.

The Center publishes monographs and books covering various aspects of Lutheran church music.

The Center maintains a dynamic website whose features include devotions, presentations, oral histories, biographical essays, resource recommendations, and conversations on various topics in worship and church music.

The Center's Founders Group includes Linda and Robert Kempke, Nancy and Bill Raabe, and Waldemar B. Seefeldt whose significant monetary gifts initiated the Center and have, along with the gifts of many others, sustained its momentum.

The Center's Advisory Board includes James Freese, Scott Hyslop, Linda Kempke, Jonathan Kohrs, Nancy Raabe, Carl Schalk, Steven Wente, and Paul Westermeyer.

Barry L. Bobb serves as its volunteer director.

You can follow news about the Center on Facebook and subscribe to its free e-newsletter.

To learn more about the Center, go to http://cuchicago.edu/about-concordia/center-for-church-music

Preface

When Carl Schalk invited me to present a lecture on Luther Reed at the annual Lectures in Church Music at Concordia University Chicago, he said that most students and many musicians these days probably no longer know Reed's work and that those who care about the Lutheran Church in North America ought to know something about the man and his accomplishments. He suggested as a topic "something like 'Luther Reed: A New Appraisal.'"

Those who have little regard for the role of the liturgy in the life of the Church have been fond of dismissing those who had a deep interest in the subject as really belonging to another tradition. Luther Reed's concern for artistic beauty and for the proprieties of manners and dress and language gave him to such eyes an Anglican inclination. The dismissive classification accorded Paul Zeller Strodach[1], because of his familiarity with Latin and German liturgical and devotional traditions, Roman Catholic leanings. Reed's successor as professor of liturgics, hymnology, and church architecture at the Philadelphia Seminary, George Rise Seltzer[2], who by his vast store of recondite learning and expression puzzled many of his students, was by default put in the Eastern Orthodox tradition, the least apt of the three characterizations. Such facile compartmentalization is not helpful. It cannot accurately portray those whom it confines in such narrow boxes, nor does it encourage those who hold such a limited view to increase and expand their understanding of the nature and possibilities of Christian life.

This monograph, faithful to Dr. Schalk's suggested title, attempts to present a rounded portrait of Luther Reed in an effort to look at and listen to and learn from one who was in his time and who is still one of the giants of the Lutheran tradition.

What is presented in these pages, therefore, is not a revolutionary appraisal of Luther Reed but a deepened respect for the breadth as well as the depth of his life and teaching and writing. Perhaps this monograph will encourage the continuation of his influence to a new generation and encourage them to seek the best of the Church's liturgical understanding and practice and thus, like Reed, be strengthened in a life of selfless service.

Luther Reed

The Legacy of a Gentleman and a Churchman

It was the spring of 1960 in the Krauth Library of the Lutheran Theological Seminary at Philadelphia. An angry shout came from the office of the long-retired president of the seminary who was reading his mail. "Damn. Damn! How could anyone be so damned stupid?" It was the voice of Luther Reed, and, it turned out, the venerable and usually mild-mannered gentleman was talking about himself.

The name Luther Reed is, to many perhaps, no longer familiar. You may know (as you should) his great work, *The Lutheran Liturgy* (1947, revised edition1960). If in your daily prayer you use, as you should, the four-volume *For All the Saints* and if, as you should, you attend to the Fourth Reading each day, you have read in volume II (pp. 885-886) Reed's comments on the distinctiveness of the Lutheran Liturgy, and in that same volume (vol. II, pp. 318-319) you will find a prayer written by him that is a good introduction to the man, his formation by the liturgical heritage of the Church, his aspirations, and his character.

Almighty God, whose love and power are shown in Thy creation and in the lives of men, and whose Providence appoints our time and place in this world: Help us by Thy Spirit's guidance to worship Thee in the beauty of holiness, to seek truth sincerely, and to desire goodness in all humility; so that, ever trusting in Thy sure mercy and forgiveness, we may know the fullness of life, perceive Thy purposes for ourselves, and use the talents Thou hast given us in the service of others; through Him who loved us and gave Himself for us, even Jesus Christ, Thy Son, our Lord.[3]

For Luther Reed the classical triad of the beautiful, the true, and the good, taken together, teach us the fullness of life, reveal to us why we have been set in this specific time and place, and point us to unselfish service of others. All three elements are necessary.

When he was called upon to give an extempore prayer, Reed was able, because of his deep grounding in classical liturgical formulations, to come up with a prayer (like the example just provided) in proper traditional collect form with an appropriate address, an antecedent reason leading to a petition, a statement of the desired result, and a concluding doxology. The traditional collect form encouraged clear thinking and concise expression. For Reed, the liturgy was not just for formal public worship but was a guide and pattern for our whole spiritual life, indeed for all that Christian people do.

In his later years he wore a hearing aid, and that increasing deafness surely influenced a prayer he composed for the collection *Collects and Prayers for Use in Church* (1935) "For the Deaf".

O Lord Jesus Christ, Whose compassion encompassed every infirmity of body and soul, and Who didst touch the ears of one that was deaf and opened them: Let Thy grace, we beseech Thee, rest upon all who suffer the loss of hearing; and grant that while they may not hear the sound of laughter or of music with the bodily ear, their hearts may ever know Thy loving voice, be joyous with Thy praise and be attuned to Thy Spirit; and find that harmony with Thyself which shall give them happiness in this life and joy in Thy presence for evermore; Who livest and reignest with the Father and the Holy Spirit, ever One God, world without end.[4]

The prayer is built on a pleasing interplay of music and laughter, harmony and joy, looking beyond the afflictions of this world to the satisfying pleasures of the next.

Luther Dotterer Reed[5] was born March 21, 1873 in North Wales, Pennsylvania, a borough to the northwest of Philadelphia, where his father was serving as pastor of St. Peter's Church. His musically and poetically inclined father, Ezra Leiss Reed (1842-1911) was a graduate of Franklin and Marshall College in the class of 1865 and of the new Lutheran Theological Seminary at Philadelphia in the class of 1868, the fourth class to graduate from that newly-established Confessional seminary of the General Council. The family (the father, his wife Annie Linley Reed, and their two children) moved often. The elder Pastor Reed served St. Peter's, North Wales from 1868-1873, St. John's in Center Square, Pennsylvania for a year, 1868-1869; Christ Church, Trenton, New Jersey for a year, 1873-1874; four years at First Church, Selinsgrove and Zion Church, Kratzerville, Pennsylvania, 1875-1879; St. Paul's Minersville for a year, 1879-1880; Holy Trinity, Lancaster as assistant pastor for a year, 1880-1881; then settled down at Christ Church, Lancaster, 1880-1892; St. John's in Catawissa, Pennsylvania, 1892-1897; and finally at Christ Church, West Newton, Pennsylvania for ten years, 1897-1907.

A glimpse into Luther Reed's formative years is provided in a prayer he wrote for use by students and young people generally. The prayer reveals his sense of grateful dependence on what others have done to assist him in his development and to instill in him a clear sense of duty and service.

Almighty God, who art the author of every good and perfect gift, and who hast given unto men the gifts of love and the spirit of service: Make me conscious of Thy Providence and of the privileges which the gifts and sacrifices of others have provided for me; and help me so to use these years of preparation that I may go forth to meet the responsibilities and satisfactions of life with a pure heart, a glad and disciplined mind and a ready will in the service of others; through Him who is the Lord and the servant of all, even Jesus Christ, Thy Son, my Saviour.[6]

We see here one who is conscious of what the family and community have done for him and who therefore looks forward to the responsibilities as well as the satisfactions of life.

Luther Reed graduated (at age 19) from his father's alma mater, Franklin and Marshall College, in Lancaster, Pennsylvania, in 1892 and received his M.A. in 1897; he graduated from the Philadelphia Seminary in 1895. He was later awarded a number of honorary degrees: a D.D. from Muhlenberg College and another from Thiel College, both in 1912: A.E.D. [doctor of architectural engineering] from Muhlenberg in 1936; L.H.D. from Wittenberg College in 1957; and a Litt.D. from Augustana College in 1958.

An important part of Reed's spiritual formation was the influence of his alma mater. Franklin and Marshall College was a merger (in 1853) of Franklin College, founded in Lancaster in 1787 by Lutheran and Reformed pastors, the first president of which was a son of Henry Melchior Muhlenberg, Gotthilf Heinrich Ernst Muhlenberg, and Marshall College, founded in Mercersburg, Pennsylvania, in 1836. The latter institution attracted a distinguished faculty that gave rise to what came to be called Mercersburg Theology, a movement that originated in the German Reformed Church in the mid-nineteenth century in opposition to the emotionalism and rationalism of the time and emphasized the teaching of the Reformers in relation to patristic and subsequent thought. The leaders of the movement were John Williamson Nevin (1803-1886), president of Marshall College 1841-1853 and of Franklin and Marshall College 1866-1876, and Philip Schaff (1819-1893) Nevin's colleague on the Marshall faculty who later joined the faculty of Union Theological Seminary in New York. Their theology emphasized a more sacramental approach to Christianity than was common in the Protestant churches of the time and encouraged liturgical recovery and renewal. The chief influence on the Mercersburg Theology came not from the Oxford Movement in the Anglican Church but from contemporary thought in Germany (Schaff was educated at Tübingen, Halle, and Berlin.) Surely Luther Reed imbibed this theology during his college years as did his father before him, and it helped shape his thought and life.

In Reed's senior year at seminary, 1895, when most courses consisted largely of dictation and memorization, Henry Eyster Jacobs organized a research course in liturgics. He would propose a topic, and then students did research in the library, presenting the results of their work at a weekly seminar. Luther Reed, Jacobs notes in his memoirs, "could not get enough, but studied day and night."[7] It was Luther Reed's intention to remain at the seminary after his ordination to pursue independent study under Dr. Jacobs and to further his already proficient musical knowledge and ability by studying with Philadelphia musicians. But this was not to be. He had spent Holy Week and Easter at Emmanuel Church in the Manchester section of what was then Allegheny City (now the North Side of Pittsburgh) which was without a pastor. At the urging of the Pennsylvania Superintendent of Missions, William Alfred Passavant, Jr., Reed abandoned his personal plans and, after his ordination by the Ministerium of Pennsylvania, June 10, 1895, accepted the call from Emmanuel's. It was not a propitious beginning for one who was to become the liturgical leader of the Lutheran Church in America. Emmanuel's Church was a tiny, struggling chapel in an unpromising section of the city. The year after Pastor Reed resigned, the church left its original location and moved to the suburban community of Bellevue. The congregation, like most, especially beyond the Allegheny Mountains, had little sense of what it meant to be the Church. Reed described the small mission as ". . . a little frame chapel, no choir, no vestments, no liturgy. The pulpit was the center, on a little platform, and down in front of it on the lower level was a 'lunch table' which served as the Communion table. There was no cross, and the pastor wore street clothes."[8] When Reed left that parish seven years later, however, there was the *Church Book* for the liturgy and hymns, a black gown, a choir directed by himself, and an altar guild which made paraments for the church.

One cannot help being awed by the remarkable, almost unbelievable patience of the liturgically-minded pastors of that period. Even the great Adolph Spaeth at St. Johannis in Philadelphia ran into trouble when it came to furnishing his new building. The architect's drawings, accepted by the vestry, showed the Roman style with the round arch, "the chancel furnished in correct churchly taste, with an elevated altar back against the wall, and a pulpit at the side." But, Dr. Spaeth reports, "I had a curious experience with my good vestrymen. To those born and bred Germans and Swabians the architect's drawing was 'not American enough!' They demanded a pulpit in the centre of a great platform, filling up the entire altar niche, and back of it a 'real American' red plush-upholstered sofa must be placed! For the altar the architect was not even allowed to make a drawing. 'I will attend to that myself' said our good President, a skilled carpenter, but one who had never made any study of ecclesiastical art or architecture. The result was what might have been expected. Under the fantastic curved rococo lines of the pulpit stood a poor little cupboard, called an altar, but on which there was no room for the communion vessels until a leaf was added, so that, like a kitchen table, it could be made larger when necessary! Twenty-five years I put up with this offense to my own churchly taste and that of others. . . ."[9] Such remarkable pastoral patience was apparently necessary at the time, and it laid for us who came afterward with less patience a solid foundation on which to build.

Reed's parish reflected the general state of liturgical life in Lutheran churches in Western Pennsylvania at the time. The historic liturgy was not generally honored. (There was unrest at First Church, Pittsburgh, when in the later 1840s the pastor, William A. Passavant, tried to introduce the recitation of the Lord's Prayer and the Apostles' Creed). Vestments of any kind were practically unknown; even the black "clerical robe" was suspect as evidence of Roman leanings; revivals were conducted by a number of Lutheran congregations. Lutheranism at the time had all the characteristics of what James White has called "the Frontier Tradition."[10] Nonetheless, there were not a few who were interested in the liturgical inheritance of the Lutheran tradition, and so, during the 1898 annual meeting of the Pittsburgh Synod of the General Council, held in Pittsburgh, Reed suggested the formation of a Lutheran Liturgical Association. At that synod a preliminary meeting on September 3, 1898 drew twenty or more clergymen. One month later, October 3, 1898, a permanent organization was brought into being at First Church, Pittsburgh. A constitution was adopted and officers were elected. Luther Reed was president, Elmer F. Krauss vice-president, R. Morris Smith secretary-treasurer, and George Gongaware, pastor of First Church, bore the splendid title *archivarius*. The same officers were re-elected every succeeding year until the Association discontinued its operations in 1905 when the president urgently requested to be relieved of the duties of his office. In its first year the Association had seventy-five subscribers; in its last year there were nearly four hundred drawn from twenty-two states and the District of Columbia, four provinces of Canada, and India, representing five general bodies of the Church. The association met often. Fifty-one regular conventions were held during the seven-year lifetime of the organization "at which many valuable papers, prepared by many of the best-informed men in all parts of the Church" were presented. In addition to these meetings in the afternoon, always in the Sunday School chapel of the First Church, evening sessions were held monthly in one of the churches in the Pittsburgh area "to which the congregations of the city were especially invited. At these sessions Vespers were read and various liturgical subjects of a more generally popular nature were discussed." It was the publication and dissemination of these papers that the Association found "its most important work—the work that is of permanent value to the Church." The lasting monument to the Association and its work are the *Memoirs of the Lutheran Liturgical Association* gathered in in two books. (Each year's collected papers are identified as a separate volume; the first book of the *Memoirs* includes "volumes" I and II, the second book includes "volumes" III-VII.) Reed is accurate in his evaluation of the collection: "The papers are undoubtedly of very unequal merit. Some are quite brief; others are exhaustive treatises which embody the fruits of years of earnest and patient investigation. Altogether they unquestionably comprise the most extensive and most valuable collection of Lutheran liturgical literature in the English language. . . . [T]hey have certainly proved of inestimable service to pastors and laymen in many parishes."[11] The inclusion of the laity among those influenced by the work of the Association is noteworthy.

The essays, while focusing on the liturgy in America, also included studies of the Swedish, Norwegian, Danish, and Icelandic liturgies. The range of the essays is impressive:

Volume I

The Fundamental Principles of Christian Worship (J. C. F. Rupp)

Our Distinctive Worship—The Common Service and Other Liturgies, Ancient and Modern (Luther Reed)

The Significance of Liturgical Reform (Edward Traill Horn)

The Sources of the Morning Service of the Common Service (R. Morris Smith)

Volume II

The Architecture of the Chancel (Elmer F. Krauss)

The Significance of the Altar (W. E. Schramm)

The Swedish Liturgies (N. Forslander)

Altar Linen (Luther Reed)

The Sources of the Minor Services (R. Morris Smith)

The History of the Liturgy of the Lutheran Church in Denmark (Edmund Belfour)

Thematic Harmony of Introit, Collect, Epistle, and Gospel (David H. Geissinger)

Art in Worship (Jeremiah F. Ohl)

Volume III

The Administration of the Lord's Supper in Different Ages of the Church (G. S. Seaman)

The Liturgical History of Confirmation (C. Theodore Benze)

The Church and the Liturgy (Charles M. Jacobs)

The Church Prayer (C. Armand Miller)

The Value of Liturgical Study for Organists (Gomer C. Rees)

A General Survey of the Book of Common Prayer (Samuel A. Bridges Stopp)

Means of Liturgical Reform (T. W. Kretschmann)

Liturgical Education of the Church's Youth (R. E. McDaniel)

The Sacrificial Idea in Christian Worship (G. F. Spieker)

The Place of Liturgy in the Church's Thought, Life, and Art (John A. W. Haas)

The Liturgical History of Baptism (H. S. Gilbert)

Volume IV

The Liturgical Influence of the Lesser Reformers (C. Theodore Benze)

The Ecclesiastical Calendar (Nathan R. Melhorn)

Luther's Liturgical Writings (Earnest Anton Trabert)

The Pericopes (Adolph Spaeth)

Liturgical Development in the Period of the Reformation (Edward Traill Horn)

The Liturgical Deterioration of the Seventeenth and Eighteenth Centuries (Jeremiah F. Ohl)

Liturgy and Doctrine (David H. Geissinger)

Early American Lutheran Liturgies (D. M. Kemerer)

The Liturgy of the Icelandic Church (F. J. Bergmann)

Volume V

The Liturgical Influence of Gregory the Great (A. L. Ramer)

The Function of the Minister in Divine Worship (Elmer F. Krauss)

A Laity Liturgically Well-informed (A. B. Markley)

The Significance of Symbolism and its Employment in the Service of the Church   (George J. Gongaware)

The Collects (Samuel A. Bridges Stopp)

The Fundamental Principles of Divine Service (G. W. Mechling)

Regulations and Customs Pertaining to the Use of the Sacraments (Ira M. Wallace)

Liturgical Accuracy and Spirituality (H. Douglas Spaeth)

Volume VI

Contributive Influences Noted in the History and Structure of the Liturgy (W. A. Lambert)

Remarks on Some of Our Liturgical Classics (Edward Traill Horn)

Preaching and the Day (Paul Zeller Strodach)

Christian Worship in the Apostolic Age (Charles M. Jacobs)

The Liturgical History of Confession and Absolution (James F. Lambert)

The Sacramental Idea in Christian Worship (Adolph Spaeth)

Paraments of the Lord's House (G. U. Wenner)

Volume VII

Liturgical Colors (Paul Zeller Strodach)

Consecration (G. U. Wenner)

The Liturgical Use of the Creeds (John W. Horine)

The Liturgy of the Norwegian Lutheran Church (E. Kr. Johnsen)

Christian Worship in the First Post-Apostolic Age (Charles M. Jacobs)

The Application of Lutheran Principles to the Church Building (Edward Traill Horn)

The Bidding Prayer, Litany, and Suffrages (Charles Krauth Fegley)

The Use of Stained Glass in Ecclesiastical Architecture (Elmer F. Krauss)

Sacred Monograms—The Chrisma and the Holy Name (Edwin F. Keever)

Even after the passage of more than a century the collection continues to make fascinating reading and is a testimony to the leadership of the President of the Association. Those familiar with later nineteenth- and early twentieth-century American Lutheran history will recognize many familiar names among the list of authors of these papers.

It was during his first pastorate that Luther Reed made contacts that were to enrich the church on this continent. He found a kindred spirit in the pastor of the First English Lutheran Church in downtown Pittsburgh, David Harrison Geissinger, who was a friend of his father's, and was often invited to Pastor Geissinger's home. Through him Reed was introduced to two laymen who had a deep interest in worship, liturgy, and especially church music: Frank Weyman and Harry Archer.

The first of these, Benjamin Franklin Weyman (1842-1919), a prosperous manufacturer of tobacco products and holder of a patent on Copenhagen snuff, was, like his father, a remarkably devout and extraordinarily generous member of First English Lutheran Church, Pittsburgh. B. Frank Weyman, as he was known, was impressed with the ability and promise of the young pastor in the city across the Allegheny River and was soon to offer his continuing encouragement and support.

While he was pastor of Emmanuel's Church, Luther Reed took music lessons from Harry G. Archer (1866-1956), a graduate of what is now Carnegie Mellon University who had studied organ and piano in Berlin and described by Reed as "the best-equipped church musician in Pittsburgh at the time."[12] For seventeen years B. Frank Weyman as director of music and Harry G. Archer as organist worked together at the First Church to develop and enrich the tradition of excellence in church music, a tradition that continues to flourish in that parish. When Weyman and Archer both resigned from their positions in May of 1909, the vestry of First Church in a resolution said of B. Frank Weyman, "Appreciating the value and sacredness of the historic Church Music, and that the musical setting of the services of our Church has been brought to a high standard of excellence by Mr. Weyman, who has for a number of years taken full charge of the music in our congregation, bearing himself the greater part of the expense for the sole purpose of developing a common setting of music to our Common Service throughout the Lutheran Church, which he has also put in printed form and which is now available, and realizing that what he has accomplished has been possible only through a large and constant expenditure of thought, time and money, which can never be requited or adequately recognized, we, the Council of the First Lutheran Church, Pittsburgh, hereby record our heartfelt gratitude for his invaluable services to our congregation as well as to the entire Lutheran Church." The church council's resolution concerning the work of Harry Archer declared, "Whereas after a period of seventeen years of faithful service as Organist of this Congregation, Mr. Harry G. Archer has resigned the position in order to pursue his professional studies abroad, be it resolved, that we hereby express our cordial appreciation of the eminent ability and constant devotion with which he has filled this office, and that we gratefully recognize the distinguished service which he has rendered to the cause of Lutheran Service music."[13]

Archer and Reed had become fast friends, and Archer proposed that Reed join him in producing a ground-breaking work, *The Psalter and Canticles pointed for chanting to the Gregorian Psalm tones with a Plain Song setting for the Order of Matins and Vespers, accompanying harmonies and tables of proper Psalms for the use of Evangelical Lutheran Congregations* (1897). This work led naturally to setting the principal liturgy of the Lutheran Common Service and the other liturgical texts to Gregorian chant, making available to a broader audience what Harry Archer had introduced at First Church. Their book was *The Choral Service Book containing the authentic plain song intonations and responses of the Order of Morning Service, the order of Matins and Vespers, the Litany, and the Suffrages of the Common Service for the use of Evangelical Lutheran Congregations with accompanying harmonies for organ,* published in 1901. The book has a substantial preface of 41 pages and a six-page bibliography of books on plainsong owned by the two editors. The volume is handsomely produced, with rubrics printed in red and with abundant illuminated capitals. Behind the elaborate presentation is surely the support and generosity of B. Frank Weyman. A third book by the diligent pair was *Season Vespers containing the full text of the Vesper service with a hymn of invocation, the authentic music of the responses and of the proper antiphons, Psalms, and canticles for every season of the Church year, and the authentic music of the Litany and the suffrages with accompanying harmonies for organ* published in 1905.

At the turn of the twentieth century Reed, who had been reading the work of German liturgists such as Theodor Kliefoth's *Liturgische Abhandlungen* and Georg Rietschel's two-volume *Lehrbuch der Liturgik,* concluded that he ought to visit Europe and see for himself what was happening and to meet the men whose work he had been reading. In 1902 he was granted a leave of absence for nine months and, with the support of Frank Weyman, set sail for Europe. He enrolled for a semester at the University of Leipzig, where Rietschel was a professor. With letters of introduction in hand from Henry Eyster Jacobs, John A. W. Haas, Adolph Spaeth, and Jeremiah Ohl, on weekends he travelled to many places to visit libraries and to talk with those who were working to restore the historic liturgy and its music: Professors Reitschel and Hauck at Leipzig, Kantor Bruno Roethig of St. John's Church, Gustav Schreck, Kantor of St. Thomas Church. During the five months he spent in residence he filled fifteen notebooks with material. Two months more were spent in Scandinavia and another two in England. He returned to his parish confident that his real education had begun.[14]

Reed was pastor of Emmanuel Church from 1895 until 1903, and then for a year, 1903-1904, he was pastor of Holy Trinity Church in Jeanette, a community just to the east of Pittsburgh. His acceptance of the call to Holy Trinity was influenced in part by the promise of a slight increase in his yearly salary of $800 that might allow him to consider marriage. On June 2, 1906, in St. Michael's Church, Germantown (Philadelphia), where he had been organist during his seminary days and where he was to be a member after his return to the seminary, Luther Reed married Catherine Ashbridge, a fifth generation member of the parish. She was involved in many charitable works and was to be the "guiding spirit" of the Women's Auxiliary of the Philadelphia Seminary, an organization that was to provide invaluable support to the seminary.

Frank Weyman's generosity and high regard for Luther Reed were further demonstrated in 1906 when an anonymous offer of $50,000 was made by "a friend of the seminary (who does not desire his name to be known) for the erection on the campus of the Philadelphia Seminary a library building to be known as the Krauth Memorial Library." Three conditions were attached to the gift: (1) that the donor's name not be revealed, (2) that the library be a memorial to Charles Porterfield Krauth, the most accomplished American Lutheran theologian of the nineteenth century, who had been one of the original professors at the Philadelphia Seminary when it was founded to counter the Protestant drift of the seminary at Gettysburg, who was concurrently professor of moral philosophy at the University of Pennsylvania, and who for four years had been Frank Weyman's beloved pastor at First Church Pittsburgh; and (3) that Luther D. Reed serve as the generous donor's representative in the planning of the building. The Dean of the seminary, Henry Eyster Jacobs, and Adolph Spaeth of the faculty served with Dr. Reed as the donor's representatives. When Dr. Spaeth, who found the original plans too conventional, persuaded the committee to enlarge the scope of the project and to build something characteristically Lutheran, embodying the idea of *Ein feste Burg*, "a symbol in stone of the character of the great and honored man whose name it bears; power and strength combined with a noble refinement and elegance,"[15] the generous donor, still known only to his three representatives, responded with another $50,000 gift. The Krauth Memorial Library was completed in 1908, twenty-five years after the death of the man it honors. B. Frank Weyman died in 1919, and only then was his name revealed: Luther Reed made it known in an essay for the *Lutheran Church Review*, "A Benefactor of the Church: B. Frank Weyman." Luther Reed was the director of the Krauth Library from 1906 until 1950. The "generous donor" made further contributions in support of the library; the director himself raised a further $30,000 from alumni and interested laity.

In addition to his work as director of the library, Reed was instructor for a year, 1910-1911, and then professor of "Liturgics, including Church Music and Hymnology" from 1912 until 1945, the first professor of liturgics at a Protestant seminary in the United States. When President Charles Jacobs died in the spring of 1938, Professor Reed as "the member of the faculty longest connected with the seminary" was appointed acting president "pending the election of a successor to Dr. Jacobs." In the following year, at the age of 66, he was elected president of the seminary. He served that capacity, as well as continuing as director of the Krauth Library from 1939 to 1945 and as president emeritus from 1945 until his death. His connection with the seminary had spanned almost half of its history. He had personally known all but three of its professors. He said that his election was "to an office to which I had never aspired and for whose duties I was unprepared and, in my own judgment, unqualified."[16]

Luther Reed was widely recognized as an authority on liturgics, hymnology, and Church architecture. He was the secretary of the joint committee on the *Common Service Book* (published in 1917) and chairman of the two joint commissions which prepared the *Common Service Book's* successor, the *Service Book and Hymnal* (published in 1958). He was, as we have already heard, founder and president of the Lutheran Liturgical Association. He was a member of all the liturgical and musical boards of the Lutheran Church and beyond:

- the *Church Book* committee of the General Council, 1907-1917;
- the *Common Service Book* Committee of the United Lutheran Church in America, 1918-1958;
- the Committee on Church Music of the United Lutheran Church in America, 1918-1930;
- the Committee on Church Architecture of the United Lutheran Church in America, 1918-1948;
- the Consulting Committee of the Department of Worship of the United Lutheran Church in America, from 1955;
- the Joint Commission on the Common Hymnal, 1944-1958;
- the Joint Commission on the Liturgy, 1945-1958;
- the Commission on Worship of the Federal Council of Churches, 1932-1950;
- the Department of Worship of the National Council of Churches, 1950-.

He was also president of the Church Music and Liturgical Arts Society, president of the Associated Bureau of Church Architecture in the United States and Canada, and for many years vice-president of the Hymn Society of America. He was made an honorary member of the American Guild of Organists and of the Church Architectural Guild of America.

In his work on the *Common Service Book* he contributed a concluding stanza to Johann Michael Altenburg's hymn, beloved by the Swedes, translated by Elizabeth Rundle Charles (1858) as "Be not dismayed, thou little flock." Reed's workmanlike but undistinguished stanza, written in 1915, changed the direction of the hymn, which in its previous three stanzas had addressed the "little flock" of the Church, by appending a prayer to Christ.

Amen, Lord Jesus, hear our cry;
Stir up Thy power, come from on high,
    Defend thy congregation;
So shall Thy Church, through endless days,
Give thanks to Thee and chant Thy praise
    In joy and adoration.[17]

The hymn was continued in the 1958 *Service Book and Hymnal* but in a version of Robert Bridges' translation.

A more substantial hymn with both text and tune by Luther Reed was included in the *Service Book and Hymnal* (no. 353). In his book *Worship: A Study of Corporate Devotion* (1959) Dr. Reed described the origin of the hymn. "A hymn of trust for the nation and the church suggested by Ps. 31:15, 'My times are in thy hand.' At a resort in the Adirondacks in the summer of 1950, a group gloomily discussed national, social, and religious problems of the hour. The author suggested that we might take courage if we had the faith of the Psalmist. Retiring to his room, he wrote this hymn."[18]

O God of wondrous grace and glory,
    Whose law is love, whose love is life;
We worship thee, we bow before thee,
    In days of calm, in hours of strife.
In thee we trust; bless thou our land;
    Our times are in thy hand.

Strong Son of God, who livest ever,
    Whom death and hell could not contain,
Who stooped to serve, yet reignest ever,
    Uphold the right; let truth remain.
Forgive our sins; our lives command;
    Our times are in thy hand.

O Holy Spirit, pure and mighty,
  Whose breath revives the souls of men;
Cleanse thou our hearts, inspire us rightly
  To live, and learn, and love again.
We would not build on sinking sand;
  Our times are in thy hand.

O God, whose grace and power supernal
  Endure, though time itself decay;
Our strength renew, with life eternal
  Crown all who seek and find the way.
Thy word, O God, the Spirit's sword,
  Give peace in our time, O Lord.

To the tune he wrote for his words Reed gave the name "Mount Airy" in tribute to the seminary with which he had long been associated, located in the Mount Airy section of northwestern Philadelphia.

A lifetime of study and in particular his work on the joint committee that prepared the *Common Service Book* had laid the groundwork for his *magnum opus*, his monumental study, *The Lutheran Liturgy: A Study of the Common Service of the Lutheran Church in America.* It was published in 1947 and antedated by three years the Episcopal counterpart written by Massey Hamilton Shepherd, Jr., *The Oxford American Prayer Book Commentary.* Moreover, the book did not emerge from Reed's researches alone but was based on the extensive scholarship of the entire faculty of the Philadelphia Seminary, especially in its early decades.[19]

Reed's massive study provided a history of the liturgy of the Church from apostolic times, its adaptation in the Reformation period, its deformation under Pietism and Rationalism, and its recovery in the nineteenth century. It was an invaluable compendium, for no one knew so many of the Lutheran liturgists as did Reed. The great book further presented a detailed commentary on each part of the liturgical text of the Common Service. The book and its author regarded the 1888 Common Service, prepared by representatives of three general bodies of the Lutheran Church in North America (the General Council, the General Synod, and the General Synod South) and approved by other bodies since that time (notably the Augustana Synod and the Missouri Synod) as the typical and representative Liturgy of the Lutheran Church in the United States. Secondly the book and its author believed that the Common Service, based upon a "consensus of the pure Lutheran liturgies of the sixteenth century," was the most highly developed expression of the historic Lutheran liturgy of any time or place. Thirdly, the book and its author believed that as one of the three great liturgies of the Western Church (Roman, Anglican, and Lutheran), it is rewarding to study these comparatively, noting points of similarity and difference to reveal distinctive features of each.

The introductory chapter bears the title "The Mind of the Church," and indicates the approach. The liturgy is not something that individuals are free to make up or adapt as they please but is a reflection of the larger consciousness and experience and inheritance of the entire Christian community.

The historical section, in ten chapters, traces the development of the liturgy of the Church, its Lutheran reform, and its history in America from the time of Henry Melchior Muhlenberg. The detailed commentary that follows, in twenty-one chapters, examines the background and text of every part of The Service of Holy Communion, Matins and Vespers, the Litany, the Morning and Evening and General Suffrages. The sources and original texts of all the collects and all the prayers are provided. Three chapters give a comparative study of the propers of the Church Year (Introit, Collect, Epistle, Gradual, Gospel) as they are found in the three Western rites. Practical directions and suggestions conclude each part of the service that help the reader understand not only how to do it but how it should be understood. An appendix provides the text of the Liturgy of St. John Chrysostom, a comparative table of the liturgical text of the Roman, Anglican, and Lutheran rites, and extracts from various Eucharistic prayers. A glossary of liturgical and musical terms and an extensive bibliography of more than three hundred fifty entries conclude the volume.

The book, for all its justifiable pride in what had been accomplished, does not regard the Common Service as a finished product.

Chapter XIX, "Recension of the Canon," critically examines the unique deficiency of Luther's orders that departed from universal usage and outlines the elements that a Eucharistic prayer should include. The chapter concludes with "a proposed form" drawn from classic sources (the Apostolic Constitutions, the Liturgy of St. John Chrysostom, the Liturgy of St. Basil, the Gallican Missal, the Liturgy of St. James, the Roman Missal, the Scottish Presbyterian Book of Common Order of 1940, and the Swedish rite of 1942.) This proposed prayer, in a revised form, was to become the Eucharistic prayer of thanksgiving in the *Service Book and Hymnal* of 1958 and in the Spanish-language *Culto Cristiano* of the LCMS and was included as Eucharistic prayer III in the Ministers' Edition of the *Lutheran Book of Worship* of 1978 and as prayer 1 in *Evangelical Lutheran Worship* (2006).

The great book *The Lutheran Liturgy* bore a lovely dedication to the author's wife, who had died after "patient suffering" July 28, 1942. The dedication was printed the shape of a cross.

In
Loving
Remembrance
+
CATHARINE ASHBRIDGE REED
+
Dear
Companion
In the way
Whose faith
And courage
Climbed the
Steep ascent
Whose love
And service
Rejoiced
In the vale.

The tender remembrance is a testimony not only to Catharine Reed but to her husband as well.[20]

The first edition of *The Lutheran Liturgy* served as a companion to the *Common Service Book*. When most of the Lutheran bodies in North America came together in the hope of fulfilling the dream of Henry Melchior Muhlenberg of "one church, one book," the result was the *Service Book and Hymnal* of 1958. Reed promptly and thoroughly revised his book to focus on the Common Service in its new form, which came to be called the Common Liturgy. The revised edition is undated (still bearing the copyright date of 1947), but it was published in 1960.[21]

By the middle of the twentieth century the liturgical renewal that Luther Reed had championed since before the beginning of the century had begun to bear fruit. In 1959 he published *Worship: A Study of Corporate Devotion.* It was dedicated "To ministers, organists, and all others whose privilege and responsibility it is to order the corporate worship of the Church." An introductory section (one chapter) examined The Spirit of Worship. The second section (eight chapters) examined the church building, the church year, the church service, and the Common Liturgy and the Common Hymnal. The third section (seven chapters) examined the ministry of music its history, music of the liturgy, the hymn, the choir, the organ. The fourth section (nine chapters) examined Leadership, vestments, ceremonial, the celebration of Holy Communion, the organist-choirmaster, chanting, and a concluding chapter on the liturgical movement. Sixteen black and white photographs of church buildings illustrated a subject dear to his heart: successful modern architectural achievements. The selection of photographs was "designed to show the fine work that has been done within the last few decades by American architects in designing church buildings in every part of the country. Monumental structures such as the [Episcopal] cathedrals in New York and Washington, the great university chapels at Princeton and Chicago, and the impressive Mellon Memorial [East Liberty] Presbyterian Church in Pittsburgh have not been included. Rather the effort has been to select fine parish churches of moderate size and representing all periods and styles from early Colonial to the contemporary."[22]

The exclusion of the monumental demonstrated Reed's realistic and pastoral concern for the vast majority of Lutheran congregations in North America. It may also be evidence of a besetting limitation of the Lutheran movement at least in America: a diminished sense of vision and imagination.

In his appearance, Luther Reed was small in stature, a wiry little fellow with a carefully trimmed goatee and an astonishing abundance of energy, gentle and gracious (which is what makes the opening anecdote of this essay so surprisingly amusing). Edgar S. Brown, Jr., Director of the Commission on Worship of the Lutheran Church in America, provides an example of Reed's gentlemanly grace. "At a formal dinner attended by dignitaries, both foreign and domestic, and their wives, just prior to the LWF [Lutheran World Federation] Assembly in 1957, the meal concluded with a long and all too dull series of toasts, largely of a self-congratulatory nature. Finally, Dr. Reed pushed his chair back and got to his feet. Lifting his glass he said,

> I should like to propose a toast to the ladies present:
>
> Our arms, their sure defense;
> Their arms, our recompense.
>
> There wasn't a woman present who didn't look at her husband as if to say, ". . . and it took an 84 year old widower to do it."[23]

Reed, a gentleman of culture and refinement, nonetheless possessed a Lutheran earthiness. The Ministerium of Pennsylvania at its annual synod at the Inn at Buck Hill Falls in the Pocono Mountains of Pennsylvania was debating a statement on Communion practices. During a break in the proceedings Dr. Reed, not pleased with the level and the character of the discussion, remarked for all to hear as entered the men's room, "This seems to be the only place where we all know what we are here for."

He was throughout his life nearly always dressed in a three-piece black suit with clerical collar; in his later years he favored oxford gray rather than black. One summer in the Krauth Library I noticed him in a necktie rather than clerical collar and commented on it. He explained to be it was because of the heat that he chose a cooler style of dress (dark two-piece suit, white shirt, and tie.) His attachment to proprieties could at times be infuriating. Edward Traill Horn III reports that when meetings of the commission at work on the *Service Book and Hymnal* proposed to break for dinner and then return for an evening session at 7:30, Dr. Reed would object, "What gentleman wants to eat dinner before eight o'clock?"[24]

There are a great many people, especially in the Lutheran Church, who denigrate a concern for liturgy and the allied arts as frivolous, fussy, and even funny. Reed, even more than most, suffered such opprobrium. His colleague on the faculty of the Philadelphia Seminary, Theodore Tappert, could be a very nasty man, and at times in his centennial *History of the Lutheran Theological Seminary at Philadelphia 1864-1964* he demonstrates his vindictive inclination. In that history he makes snide comments about several members of the faculty, but especially and most memorably about his teacher, colleague, and president, Luther Reed. Tappert says of him, "His ministry was interrupted several times by extended absences occasioned by physical debility, and in 1902 he spent almost a year travelling in Europe for the cultivation of his interest in church music and art. He was one of the organizers and the president (1898-1906) of the Lutheran Liturgical Association, whose *Memoirs* he edited. In 1906 he was named director of the Krauth Memorial Library, in 1911 he was elected professor, and he continued to occupy both positions until his retirement in 1945. He served as secretary of the joint committee which prepared the *Common Service Book* (1917) and as chairman of the joint commission which produced the *Service Book and Hymnal* (1958). He also served on other committees which were concerned with church music and architecture. For a score of years he was the only member of the faculty who was furnished with secretarial help and he used this effectively to promote his special interests. In his early years he edited, with Mr. H. G. Archer, a number of texts of liturgical music. Most of his literary work was published in later years. In addition to about twenty articles in church journals, he wrote *The Lutheran Liturgy* (1947; revised edition 1959) and *Worship: a Study of Corporate Devotion* (1959). During his teaching career he received the degree of D.D. in 1912 from Thiel College and Muhlenberg College, and the latter conferred on him the degree of A.E.D. in 1936." Then follows the evaluation: "Essentially romantic and mystical in temperament, Professor Reed was attracted by the old more than by the new. Neither in the classroom nor in his writings was he concerned with the way in which people in the past actually worshipped, however, for he centered his attention on selected monuments of text or form and tended to idealize them. He was more an advocate than a scholar and more an artist than a theologian. He awakened in his students an appreciation of beauty but had scant sympathy with their quest for truth. The influence he had on his students, and through them on the church as a whole, was incalculable, for he was a diligent and persistent advocate of what he considered 'good taste.'"[25] Throughout this section of the history there drifts the unpleasant cloud of condescension and indeed the air of professional jealousy.

Luther Reed was always a gentleman, but, as Edgar Brown remarks, "beneath that dignified mien there abides a stalwart warrior, able to give as well as (if not better than) he gets."[26] Reed responded to Tappert's attack with a nine-page open letter "sent to a limited circle of perhaps 150. This will include members of the faculty, the Board of Directors, and Alumni Association, the student body and a selected list of leaders in the church, who are definitely interested in the Seminary and who should know the situation here today as it really is."[27] The letter is a masterful retort and deserves to be quoted at length for it speaks volumes about the character of its author. Reed, Tappert's elder by thirty-three years, speaks as a stern but loving father to an errant son, giving praise where it is due and reprimand where it is warranted.

Ted:

What an artist you are! The El Greco type, of course, the darling of the expressionists. With your encyclopedic memory, you may recognize him under his real name, Domenico Theotocopuli, and as the master of distorted forms and twisted lines. He was a man of enormous industry, powerful conceptions and great technique. His portraits, however, were not true portraits. Every one of them revealed more of the painter than of the sitter. His contemporaries wonder whether his vision was impaired, whether he was crazy, or simply evil minded.

This seems a proper introduction to my discussion of your history of the Seminary. The term 'your history' seems particularly appropriate, as it certainly is not, in many respects, the real history of the Seminary, but a T.G. Tappert history of the Seminary. Much of it is fine and we all admire the industry, the capacity for research and for marshalling of a mass of facts and giving them sharp, solid, condensed form. Much of your book will be very valuable and we are indebted to you. The trouble is not with your assembly of facts, but with your many guesses, assumptions, and what you are pleased to call 'assessments.' For here you are dealing with human beings, and your trouble is not simply occasional error of judgment, but malevolence of spirit. You have great gifts. You use them powerfully, but much that you do is only on secular and material levels. You are not at home in the world of the spirit, the world of culture, and so far as the Seminary is concerned, in the world of churchmanship. With you, the word is 'scholarship', but the question constantly rises, 'scholarship for what'. Your mind is like an IBM computer, cold and bloodless. You are really not able to understand flesh and blood, which accounts for the distorted character of many of your 'assessments.'

Again, let me say, there is much that is good in your book. Time will correct much that is bad. For the present we will have to be content with it as a mixture of good and bad, which in fact, is just about what much of us are. I shall not attempt to review your book as a whole. I shall speak of sections in which you give your assessment of myself, and occasionally, your questionable judgment of others, as treated in the fifty or more pages I have read so far.

It is clear as daylight that while you have spoken quite brutally of some of your colleagues and some earlier professors in the seminary, you have deliberately set out to deflate, debunk, and distort me and my service in the seminary and the church. Only six persons have read your history and spoken to me about it. One had said, 'he used a stiletto, didn't he?' Another said 'he dipped his pen in acid,' and a third, 'why has he done this to you?' You certainly have set yourself up as a veritable Pontifex Maximus, who surrounds himself with a cloak of infallibility. [Tappert was a virulent anti-Catholic] In my case, you have not only distorted facts, but you seem to have set out malevolently to put me before the seminary and the church as a chronic invalid and weakling. I would indeed be the weakling you suggest if I took your statements lying down. Others whom you have defamed are in their graves and cannot defend themselves. I am still alive, thank God, and able to rise up in my own defense and give you a few 'assessments' of my own. In the several encounters I have had with you in the past you have come out second best, and I am hoping for the best in this instance.

So then, I suggest, an easy chair and a cigar, if the state of your health will permit cigars which I still enjoy. I know that at one time you were even forbidden cigarettes. I also know, as we think of the matter of health you have brought up, that at one time you were hospitalized for many weeks with a brain tumor. All of which makes me a bit concerned even now about this matter of health so far as you are concerned.

So I would suggest, sit down and listen to what I have to say and listen to my assessments. I shall not be brief and I shall not speak in anger or rancor. The first day or two after I read your book I was angry and sore. That is past, and I shall endeavor in cool and careful analysis [to] examine your El Greco type portraits and cheerfully cut you down to size—as a historian and a man.

The Seminary is very fortunate in this its centennial year in having two fine worthwhile books concerning its history and work, appear from the press. One is John

Kaufmann's [Alumni] *Biographical Record,* a fine, complete, and trustworthy work, like the man himself. The second is your book with so much of good in it, that with so many slams and slurs, guesses and assumptions, that pass for history, but are really not. And here too, as in the case of El Greco, whose portraits revealed more of the painter than of the subject, we have a picture of yourself.

Let us begin with the Krauth Memorial Library. You know quite well of the part I had in this,--that the conception and scale of building, as caring for the future as well as present needs; the necessity of setting up a staff of professionally trained library workers, and the securing of the funds which made the erection of this kind of a building possible—you know that this was my work, almost entirely so, and that without this kind of a library all the following efforts as to methods of instruction, setting up of seminars, and a graduate school, would have been impossible. You know most of these facts, since you borrowed my Memoirs [*At Eventide: Recollections and Reflections* 1959; an unpublished typescript] and I am sure, read every word of them in the two weeks you held the book. About all you say concerning the significance of the library work and my part in it, is that I was appointed the director and that for years I enjoyed having secretarial assistance, which I used to further my 'special interests', which, by the way, were the interests of the seminary and the whole church, as I was not only a professor, and in full charge of the library, but chairman of the church's Committee on Music, Committee on Architecture, Common Service Book Committee, and similar matters in the liturgical and musical field. I also represented our church in its relationship with similar organizations in other communions, such as the Federal Council's Commission on Worship, during the entire time of its existence, a member of the National Council's Commission on Worship and the Arts, etc.

Perhaps one other item should be mentioned with reference to the Krauth Memorial Library. You flatly state that Mr. Weyman had received three million dollars from the sale of his business. The only figure I ever heard in this connection was two million dollars. You state that Mr. Weyman paid my salary as director—all of which is your assumption and is not true. I came to the seminary and served it at my own expense, having received from Mr. Weyman—*prior* to all discussions about the library—a block of Japanese Government bonds which assured me of an income of a professor's salary at that time. Get this straight—this was prior to his offers in connection with the library, and in line with similar gifts to a few close friends, including Harry Archer. When he made his handsome gift to the seminary and withheld his name, and when, as I knew, Dr. Clarence Miller was paying seminary deficits and buying additional property for the institution, I also made my contribution by asking no salary when I was called to the seminary. Your assumptions are wrong and what I have said is God's truth. Dr. Miller was the only one who really knew the facts in the case and when I was elected a professor, he felt that this state of affairs was unfair to Mrs. Reed as well as myself, and upon Mrs. Weyman's death, he seized the opportunity as giving a reason for giving me a regular professor's salary. I state this as a matter of personal history to clear up a matter which I know has been obscure through all the years, and I cannot blame you too much for your statement because I believe what you have said was the general impression at the time. Now all of this, you will understand, I feel has entitled me to a better portrait of myself than you have presented to the church. I also feel that you have treated Dr. [E. Clarence] Miller, Dr. [Peter P.] Hagen [Hagan], and perhaps Mr. [B. Frank] Weyman and other devoted laymen quite shabbily. Without their generous financial and other support the seminary could not have survived, let alone advance.

Now for a few particulars, as they come to mind.

I am sure you knew that I had a semester at the University of Leipzig, and that on long week-ends for months I interviewed the leading scholars in the liturgical field in Germany and Scandinavia—church musicians, authors, church leaders, and others having to do with my 'special interests.' My time was not spent simply taking pictures so that I might give the boys "three shows a day."

Now for a few omissions of some items that occur to me, a few of which at least have been mentioned in your assessment of my work in the seminary.

- I organized an entire department in the field of Liturgics and Church Art, something unknown even to the present hour in any other Lutheran seminary in the country.

- I was archivist of the Ministerium of Pennsylvania for thirty years, got the stuff out of trunks and boxes, put the stuff on the shelves and catalogued it, so that you as my successor could build on this foundation as you so well have done.

- I finally succeeded in having a chancel built in the chapel, taking the place of a platform which intruded into the nave, and myself paid the architect's fee of $350.00 to have this done. Dr. Clarence Miller had the seminary pay one-third, the Church of the Ascension [a congregation that for many years shared the use of the chapel with the seminary] one-third, and he, himself, one-third of the major cost of this renovation. I cannot blame you for not referring to this at all, at least to my part of this, because no one knew of this.

- I was chairman of the Common Service Book Committee for thirty years, during which we bought forth, in addition to the *Common Service Book*, the nationally used *Collects and Prayers,* and various hymnals. I, myself, have helped others edit six hymnals form the Army and Navy Service Book down to the *Service Book and Hymnal* which now has three million copies in use.

- In your mention of my books you failed to include my editing of the seminary's Biographical Record, which served as the basis of John Kaufmann's much better book of this centennial year. You also forgot to mention my History of the First Lutheran Church in Pittsburgh. A handsomely illustrated work of 231 pages brought out by Lippincott.[28]

- You say positively that I published twenty articles. The library catalogue with which you are completely familiar, lists forty such articles, and my Memoirs, which you also know, has several more. Several of these articles were published in Geneva, Berlin, and Rotterdam, as well as in secular journals of importance such as the American Architect.

- You certainly know that I assembled and arranged the text for the Reformation Cantata "The City of God" in 1917 [the 400th anniversary of the Reformation], H. Alexander Matthews composing the music. This was published by Schirmer, and had its initial performance in the Academy of Music, Philadelphia, with Leopold Stowkowski conducting and the Philadelphia Orchestra and a chorus of four hundred voices which I organized from many Protestant choirs in the city.

Now a word about my wider church connections, which have received no comment in your history.

- I was a member of the Federal Council's Committee on Worship as I mentioned, and of the National Council of Churches' Department of Worship and the Arts.

- A member of the Faith and Order Commission of the World Council of Churches, writing for this a statement of the Lutheran Church's position in inter-communion.

- For ten years I was president of the Association [of] Bureaus of Church Architecture which during my presidency held annual conferences in cities as far west as Chicago and St. Louis, to say nothing of New York, Washington, Pittsburgh, and all the rest.

- I was a member of the American Guild of Organists, and the Pennsylvania Chapter made me an honorary member.

- I helped organize the principal professional organization of church architects in the country, The Church Architectural Guild of America, whose first president was Ralph Adams Cram. This splendid organization also made me an honorary member and gave me their first Conover Award.

- I have been for many years an active member of the Hymn Society of America, and this fine group also made me at various times a Fellow, and a Vice-President, which I still am.

- I am also an honorary member of the Lutheran Society for Worship, Music, and the Arts, and my portrait filled the first page, I believe it was, of their journal *Response*.

- I am a member of the editorial board of the international journal *Studia Liturgica*, published in Rotterdam, Holland.

- I was editor of the Philadelphia Seminary Bulletin for a period of seventeen years and associate editor (with Charles M. Jacobs) and business manager of the *Lutheran Church Review* for something like a dozen years.

Like St. Paul, "I am become a fool in glorying: ye have compelled me."

I mention all of this stuff to let you and others know that there were items of importance which you have deliberately passed by. You will understand that I would not have expected you to include all of this list. But you certainly have built up your shabby treatment of my record, by including two or three items.

Now for a few perhaps smaller items of omission or error:

You mention two honorary degrees that I hold. You should know from the faculty page in the seminary's catalog that I have four of these honors. Your handling of this matter is a nice example of your spirit and method. You say that 'during his teaching years' he received the two degrees mentioned, but you say nothing about the other two. This statement was perfectly correct but incomplete in 1964. How clever and subtle when you know no one will do any research on this little item.

Now for a few errors.

- The house in which I live on Boyer Street was bought by Clarence Miller from Carl Hassold for $23,500. As I recall quite clearly the property next door and in the rear of the library was bought for $10,000. These figures are correct, and your figures are incorrect.

- You state that I requested leave of absence from the seminary no less than three times to take pictures in Europe. I had only one leave of absence from the seminary. Other trips were in vacation time.

- Your assessment of Dr. [Theodore E.] Schmauk, to take one example, makes him a man of smaller size than Dr. [Henry] Offerman. The latter was my friend and neighbor for many years and I loved him, as everybody did. But no one would be more surprised than he to read your comparison of these two men and their service to the seminary and the church. This is but one of your many El Greco distortions.

Now for a few of your personal assessments as to my record in the seminary and the church, and here is where I feel you have been particularly malevolent in depicting me as a chronic invalid and a weakling. If I had been what you describe I would not be dictating this letter to you at 91 years of age. Your statement that I consulted a physician before accepting election to the presidency [of the seminary] is a case in point. Was not this a natural thing for any man of 64 to do? You have made it a point to prove your statement of poor health. You have not mentioned, of course, that my presidency exactly coincided with the period of the Second World War; that we were working around the clock with the 'accelerated program' which kept us going without vacations, and with the added problems of the Navy's Chaplain Training Program, administrative duties piled up. We made Dr. Hoh assistant to the president, an office which he filled with great competence.

You and several other members of the faculty represented me at conference meetings, etc. This is the basis for your statement that during my presidency many administrative duties were transferred to others. I have no doubt that similar procedures had to be followed in many other institutions.

Your statement that I was not particularly concerned with how people worshipped or with students' quest for truth is characteristic of your mishandling of truth and your lack of Christian spirit. What is a life-long effort to provide the church with the best possible liturgies and hymnals but a concern for truth and precisely how people worship? You cannot be expected to understand this, but the brief text of The Prayer of Thanksgiving [the Eucharistic prayer in the *Service Book and* Hymnal] in our present liturgy is a fuller and truer expression of the Gospel and the plan of salvation than is often revealed in many sermons or theological treatises. Bach's cantatas and his B-minor Mass have more Christian truth in them and more of the Gospel than some of the Confessions, such as the Smalkald Articles, which we are required to swallow—hog-skin, bindings, and metal clasps—before we can be installed as a professor in the seminary.

One trouble with you is that you travel on a single line of track, and that often narrow gauge, in the fields of theology and church history, which is important, necessary, and worthy of all praise. You fail to realize that the 'scholarship' of which you so frequently speak is found also in other areas, particularly the fields of culture and the vital matter of churchmanship. You will understand that by churchmanship I am not referring to crosses and genuflections, to candles, vestments, incense, and sanctus bells. By churchmanship I mean the whole proper life, thought, spirit, and artwork of the church—not only its worship, but its missions, its educational program, its social service, and Christian ethics. The long trains, heavily loaded with discussions of theology and church history on which you travel, never pass through the fields of culture, all unknown to you. It is, perhaps, too much to expect that you have ever read John Keats' "Ode to a Grecian Urn." His final lines say:

"Beauty is truth, truth beauty,"—that is all
Ye know on earth, and all ye need to know.

Your knowledge is vast, but it is not big enough to understand large and important areas of the church's life. When you attempt to enter these fields and make the assessments you do, this lack of knowledge really shows up. Your history has so much that is valuable, but it has so much that is to be regretted, with omissions that are glaring, that, as I have already stated, your book in this centennial year will not be nearly as important and valuable for the seminary and the church as John Kaufmann's companion volume, the Biographical Record.

And now we come to the close of what has been a warm but not too unpleasant afternoon. What I have attempted to say in self-defense has been a calm and cool assessment and not said in anger. I feel I have really dealt with you quite gently considering your provocation. And now I would suggest that you take a walk—perhaps into the wilds of Wisconsin or along the banks of the Mississippi. Or better yet, go to Mittel-Europa. I advise you to stay in this jungle and not return to the seminary. The seminary will certainly be vastly better off without your presence. If you decide not to stay in the jungle, I can see what will happen. The split in the faculty and in the student body which you and your attitudes and close associates have produced will continue and be deepened. Your efforts to have the faculty regard the seminary not as an institution of the church, working in the field of education, but as an educational institution doing something for the church but for anybody as well. You would like to have it thought of not as church school but simply as a school. You have already taken all Christian thought and sense of motivation and dedication on the students' part out of the Matriculation Service, which under your inspiration is now a mere calling of the roll. Your leadership in the faculty, which you have subtly and gradually assumed and exercised has produced an astonishing statement on Holy Communion. You finally succeeded in reducing chapel communion services from once a week to five or six times a year. This has so disgusted the student body that chapel attendance as of last semester dropped as low as eight or twelve students at times and an average of perhaps twenty-five or less out of a student body of 183.

It has entirely obliterated the seminary choir at regular chapel services. As far as regular chapel services are concerned, no such thing any longer exists. We have a splendid concert choir, but it is not in the stalls for chapel services except upon very special occasions.

If you should come back or stay, you would of course continue and build up the coffee breaks in the refectory, and you would wish them to be at the chapel hour, as a further indication of the fact that the devotional life and the spirit of worship does not deserve much consideration in the seminary's program or in the life of the students. The coffee Klatches you have so assiduously held every Friday afternoon in your own home would of course be continued as serving up your 'special interests', in building up a body of Tappert 'fans' and enriching your collection of cheap student parodies. Your persistent pushing of advanced graduate work and further degrees, etc. is diverting the seminary from its original purpose and its actual reason for being, which is primarily to prepare men for the parish ministry. I am all for graduate study and scholarship of the highest order, but this will probably never involve more than five or ten percent of our student body, and your concentration upon it is out of all proportion. You wish to produce 'little theologians' instead of dedicated pastors and practicing Christians. You have never grasped the aim of Drs. [Charles Porterfield] Krauth, H. E. Jacobs, C. M. Jacobs, Schmauk, E. T. Horn, and myself and others, to develop English Lutheranism in America, the only kind of Lutheranism that will survive in this country.

Your whole program out of which you have developed and would pursue will put the seminary, as I have repeatedly told Dr. Bagger [Henry Horneman Bagger, then the president of the seminary], behind the church and not as a leader, ahead of the church where we have always been. The recent action of the Lutheran Church in America at Pittsburgh commending weekly observances of the sacrament, which we had here at the seminary for fifteen years, shows the renewed appreciation of Holy Communion as a means of grace. The action of such congregations as Christ Church, Allentown in introducing this is a confirmation of this attitude. Even the Presbyterians in their new directory of worship express the propriety of Holy Communion at the principal service at every Lord's Day. The position which you and your associates have taken on this matter will certainly rob the Philadelphia Seminary of all claim to leadership in this vital matter.

You may feel that I have been a bit rough, but you have made it necessary for me to defend myself, and I have taken advantage of the opportunity this has presented to put before the seminary and the church my assessment of you and your work.

The concluding lines of the letter have already been quoted above in the introduction to this long quotation.

Reed's response to Tappert stands in a genre of theological retort that combines clear thinking, profound understanding, and a remarkable helping of humor. It is the same genre as Charles Porterfield Krauth's response to the vitriolic attacks by Benjamin Kurtz on the General Council and all that it stood for. In its European context, the genre became widely known in Karl Barth's 1934 book-length rejection of Emil Brunner's attempt to resuscitate natural theology with the blunt title *Nein!*

What is interesting in this multi-faceted defense is what Reed did not say. While criticizing Tappert's interest in graduate education, Reed refrained from noting that Tappert himself, like Reed and most of the older faculty, did not have an earned doctorate.

Reed's description of the marginalization of the chapel in the life of the seminary had been true for a number of years. It was an accurate description in the years I was a student at Mount Airy, 1957-1960. Morning Prayer was said not at the beginning of the day but at 10 o'clock in the morning, coffee break time. It was small wonder that many students and faculty chose the refectory rather than the chapel. This was a concern for Reed well before the provocation of Tappert's history. Reed had written in his memoirs, dated 1959, "Cultivation of the spiritual life, participation in the daily services of common worship,--these are for them [who regard only intellectual effort as the single important feature of seminary life] matters of indifference. They do not believe that it is as important for the full development of Christian personality—and particularly for students in formative years—to cultivate qualities of reverence and the spirit of worship in the community of believers as it is to learn the facts of history, systems of doctrine, grammatical forms of Greek and Hebrew, or the rules of homiletics."[29] It needs to be clearly understood that he does not denigrate the study of systematic theology and scripture and preaching, but that he is insisting on the importance, even the centrality of the spiritual life, especially for those who would be pastors of the Church. Such attention to regular worship is not only for the individual nor for effective ministry; it is required and expected primarily because each of us is a member of the body of Christ and each of us must learn what it means to live a part of that body. Reed continues (women were not yet ordained in the Lutheran Church in America), "There are spiritual values for men in the ministry, as well as for men preparing to enter it, in regular attendance at chapel services, in becoming perfectly familiar with the Church's forms and usages, in growing appreciation of what it means to be part of the Body of Christ, the Church, as it devoutly worships Almighty God." Warming to his subject, he continues, "A coffee-break is a shocking substitute for a chapel service. Yet in the hour appointed for common worship, there are those who heed not the chapel bell, but instead a cozy refectory table, build there an altar to a strange god, and worship at the shrine of Holy Coffee Pot. The steam from this idol's mouth scarce reaches the low ceiling of this retreat, while in the neighboring House of the Lord the prayers of the faithful rise like incense to the throne of heavenly grace."[30] He does not suggest compulsory chapel, for seminarians must learn self-discipline, "how to order their lives, how to make right decisions, how to seek the highest good." While he deplores the actions of those professors and students who choose coffee over chapel he knows that "the choice is, and must be, theirs."

Reed's understanding of the Christian life was notably full and rich, going far beyond what Tappert and others ridiculed as "millenary." His concern, as he said again and again, was not for the trappings of worship but for the fullness of life in Christ: worship and learning and missionary work and the service of others. His concern reached out to embrace all of society. It was not limited, as was much of the church's social concern of the time, to matters of individual morality: gambling, dancing, entertainment and sports events on Sunday, the coarsening of literature and movies. Reed's concern was larger and more inclusive. He was troubled by signs of moral and spiritual decline, social injustice, "the rising might of militarism," all of which he had observed at close hand in early twentieth-century Europe. This experience aroused his indignation then and continued in his fears for his own country. He wrote in his 1959 memoirs, "As I write these lines now, after nearly sixty years I have only to regret that many of these customs of a war-torn and weary Europe have been transferred to America and are now flourishing here with possibly greater intensity and menace in our own land and time."[31] His concern for the liturgy of the Church was no flight from reality, but rather the impetus for an engagement with the world as it is in all its thoughtless brutality.

There are those who talk a great deal about our large social obligations to the life of the world but who neglect what they can actually accomplish in their own small corner of the world, advising others what they ought to do but neglecting to do even small things themselves. Luther Reed was not one of those. Edward Traill Horn III concludes his essay "A 30th Anniversary Remembrance of the Publication of the *Service Book and Hymnal*" with a revelation. "And finally, I think it is time to reveal something entirely new. One of my duties was to serve as treasurer of the two Commissions [on the Liturgy and on the Hymnal]. The Commission on the Liturgy wanted three musical settings of the Service—one Anglican Chant in its best contemporary form, another in plainsong, another in choral form. We Lutherans could not furnish the first two. We went to Dr. Harold W. Gilbert, headmaster of St. Peter's Choir School in Philadelphia, for the Anglican Chant; and to Ernest White, faculty member at the Pius X School [for the plainsong]. Both agreed to arrange settings without charge. They did, and Dr. Reed, out of his own pocket, had me send them honoraria of $500. I think everyone else who knew that is now gone, but it should be on the record."[32] Luther Reed was ever the kind and thoughtful gentleman, who did not call attention to his own considerateness.

Among my most precious possessions is a letter I received shortly after my aunt, Helen Pfatteicher, died. It was handwritten on the letterhead the President Emeritus of the Lutheran Theological

Seminary at Philadelphia, and dated Dec. 5, 1970, the day following my aunt's death at the age of 58.

> Dear Philip: Word of your Aunt Helen's death has shocked and saddened me and I write to express my deep sympathy. You are, I believe, the only one of your family that I know now and there were so many in your family connection that I knew very well and regarded very highly. Helen, as I knew her, was a splendid specimen of Christian womanhood—capable, talented, kind, consecrated, and doing everything well—I have found her a very good friend who served her Church. Hers was a rich and distinguished service to her Lord and his Church. I am working practically blind so pardon the writing. My deep sympathy to you and to your family. Sincerely yours, Luther D. Reed.

That is the best I can do deciphering the writing of a trembling hand that several times overwrites a previous line. It was a remarkably gracious gesture by a 97 year-old, the last of a generation that had changed the Lutheran Church in this country for the better. I showed the letter to my father, Helen's brother, who was, like me, deeply moved and at the same time saddened by the writing. It was my father who had introduced me to Dr. Reed one Sunday afternoon about 1952 when we came upon him dining alone in the restaurant of Alden Park Manor in Philadelphia.

Luther Reed lived for just two more years after writing that letter of condolence. At age 99 he had expressed his desire to see one more Easter. His wish was granted: on Easter Monday, April 3, 1972, "he died in my arms," Bishop William Lazareth told me.

"A man's work has to be judged by his time," Dr. Reed remarked to Thomas Edge in an interview.[33] One might be tempted to observe that Reed had his limitations. For example, in an essay in *Response*, the Journal of the Lutheran Society for Worship, Music, and the Arts, late in his long life, in an otherwise insightful essay he defended the use of Tudor English in the liturgy by asking rhetorically, "Would you like to see and sing 'We praise you. We bless you. We worship you. We glorify you' or, at the end of all prayers, 'through our Lord Jesus Christ, your Son, who lives and reigns with You'?"[34] By the last quarter of the twentieth century it was obvious that nearly all of English-speaking Christianity had answered the question with a resounding "Yes." From the middle of the twentieth century at least, the King James translation of the Bible had been under attack. The committees preparing the *Service Book and Hymnal* were under pressure to replace the Authorized Version of the Bible with the newly-completed Revised Standard Version (1952) for the biblical readings. Among those who opposed the change was none other than the prominent President of the United Lutheran Church in America, Franklin Clark Fry ("Mr. Protestant" *Time* magazine called him when his portrait appeared on its cover), who declared, "There are two reasons why I do not like the RSV text. The first is, I know Greek. The second is, I know English."[35] Such deep attachment to the sonorous rhythms of the Authorized Version by many of the time now to most seems understandable but antiquated.

Luther Reed was surely a man of his time, but it needs also to be observed that he was in many respects ahead of his time. Indeed, at his inauguration as president of the seminary he identified "progressiveness" as the first characteristic of "the spirit of the Philadelphia Seminary."[36] The vestments he sought gently to introduce or recover, first a black gown and then cassock, surplice, and stole, became the standard dress of Lutheran clergy in the 1950s and 60s. The Eucharistic vestments he tentatively approved have in recent decades become common throughout the Lutheran churches in North America. Attention to such externals, however, would not have entirely pleased Dr. Reed. Change in vestments has little meaning without a corresponding change in understanding and a deepening of reverence. He was ever on his guard against the easy path of concentrating on ceremonial matters to the exclusion of spirituality. And spirituality for him, living the Christian life, begins at the altar but then expands from the sanctuary out into the needy and suffering world where one meets Christ in the faces and lives of his people. His concern for the broad societal and ethical implications of the liturgy has become a standard feature of modern studies of the use and significance of the Liturgy.

His progressiveness included the possibility of certain innovations. Looking ahead in 1966 to the next liturgical book he remarked, "I would encourage anything which would bring in more of an active participation by the laity, coming up from the body of the nave into the chancel to take part in the Service (e.g. an Offertory Procession). I would encourage study of that. . . . I think it would be a fine addition to the liturgy in line with its beauty and symbolism, as well as good doctrine and practical congregational participation."[37]

Tappert and others accused Reed and those with similar interests of "romanticism," as if he and those like him were inclined to escape into an idealized past that never actually existed in reality. ("Romanticism" need not be a bad word. I remember Richard John Neuhaus, at his most activist phase in his Brooklyn parish, when he was the object of a similar characterization, remarking that he saw nothing wrong with romanticism. It provided a vision of something to strive for.) For Reed, the Church's worship was, as Alexander Schmemann was later to say, "for the life of the world." He, like most of the faculty of the Philadelphia Seminary, understood and worked within a tradition of liturgical and allied scholarship and liturgical renewal that recognized the centrality of the liturgy in the life and work of the Church. They took the urban setting of the seminary as significant and were aware of the intersection of theological study with the surrounding city and its culture, problems, and needs. Christianity was to be a living faith, that is to say, a faith that is both alive and a faith that exists in intimate connection with life.

Reed's own assessment of his life was honest and remarkably accurate. In a letter dated December 27, 1954, he wrote to a long-time friend, Dr. T. Carl Whitmer of New York, who had written to him in praise of Reed's many achievements. In his reply Reed said,

> . . . somebody was unkind enough, or perhaps truthful enough, to call me an "octogeranium." I suppose the label is not a libel. The geranium is a respectable, though humble and homey sort of flower which we often find on kitchen windows. As I think of it, I've been a humdrum sort of a fellow, plodding along and trying to keep up with his more brilliant colleagues, and generally out of breath at that.

After an undistinguished parish ministry of a decade, I was catapulted into a vortex of activities for which I had little preparation and few qualifications. I became director of a technical library, though I was not a professional librarian. Then I was made a professor, though I had never had a course in pedagogy. Then president of a theological seminary, though I have never really been a theologian. In this position, I am also acting as chairman of committees and commissions galore, I have pushed around dozens of men abler than myself, without, so far as I know, ever making any of them mad.

I am not a ready writer, but a lot of people have read books and articles I have ground out with more perspiration than inspiration. (My 712 page "The Lutheran Liturgy" is in its third large printing, and I have letters from nearly a dozen foreign countries about it.) I am no musician, but I have edited half a dozen Service Books and Hymnals and the AGO [American Guild of Organists] made me an honorary member. I am no architect, but I have reviewed hundreds, perhaps a thousand, church plans and have told architects and building committees what to do. And the Church Architectural Guild of America, the top organization of specialists in this field, gave me their first Award for distinguished service at their annual meeting in Knoxville, Tenn., last winter.

. . . "I am become a fool in glorying, yet you have compelled me." As the Geranium looks back over four-fifths of a century, he simply cannot believe it, much less understand it. . . .

Forgive the foolishness. You seduced me, and in a moment of weakness I yielded to temptation. It's an old story, and it's about the only justification for my profession. There would be few penitents without preachers.[38]

There we have a record of Luther Reed's self-deprecating humor and his honest evaluation of his own limitations.

We may return to that beautifully all-encompassing collect written by Luther Reed with which we began. It is a prayer to Almighty God "whose love and power are shown in the lives" of human beings, "and whose Providence appoints our time and place in this world: Help us by Thy Spirit's guidance to worship Thee in the beauty of holiness, to seek truth sincerely, and to desire goodness in all humility; so that, ever trusting in Thy sure mercy and forgiveness, we may know the fullness of life, perceive Thy purposes for ourselves, and use the talents Thou hast given us in the service of others; through Him who loved us and gave Himself for us, even Jesus Christ, Thy Son, our Lord." It is fitting and appropriate that a prayer should gather into clear focus the life and vision and work of Luther Dotterer Reed.

Appendix

In 1935 the Common Service Book Committee of the United Lutheran Church in America produced a book called *Collects and Prayers for Use in Church*. Luther Reed, who chaired the committee and who, with Paul Zeller Strodach and Emil E. Fischer comprised the sub-committee on Collects and Prayers, contributed thirteen prayers to the collection. The expression is, of course, dated in several ways, but the prayers are nonetheless worth careful attention, giving further evidence of the depth and breadth of his piety and spirituality and also reflecting the spirit of the times in which they were composed.

It is perhaps noteworthy that there are no prayers by Dr. Reed in several categories where one might expect him to have had a special interest: The Church Building, Missions, Times and Seasons, The Church Year. That absence may perhaps reflect his modesty and reticence, his respect for the learning and gifts of other students of the liturgy of the Church.

Under the first heading in the collection, The Church, there was one prayer by Reed.

No. 20—The Church and Righteous Citizenship
    Almighty God, Who art the Ruler of the whole earth, and from Whom cometh all rule and authority among the peoples; make all who dwell in this our country mindful of Thy favor in granting us this goodly land as our heritage. Bless, we pray Thee, those whom the citizens of this country by their choice, have entrusted with the powers of government. Endue the people with the spirit of respect and willing obedience for wholesome law, and cause them to aid our

chief executives, our judges and magistrates, in maintaining peace and righteousness throughout our borders. Enable us as a people brought hither out of many kindreds and tongues and knit together now as one nation, so to love and fear Thee, the God and Father of all mankind, that we may ever strive for that obedience to Thy holy law, which shall make us a nation acceptable unto Thee, and a people among whom Thy glory may ever dwell; through Jesus Christ, Thy Son, our Lord. *Amen.*

Under the heading The Parish there were two prayers.

No. 52—*At the Time of an Election of a Pastor*

O Lord Jesus Christ, Who art the Head of Thy Body, the Church, and the Shepherd and Bishop of souls: Be present, we pray Thee, with this congregation now assembled for the purpose of calling a pastor; strengthen all hearts and minds by the purifying and enlightening power of the Holy Spirit, so that, mindful only of the welfare of this congregation and of Thy holy Church, *these Thy servants (we)* may be guided of Thee in *their (our)* decisions, and a godly and able pastor finally be chosen to minister to *them (us)* in all spiritual good, to the honor of Thy Name and the upbuilding of Thy Kingdom here among men; Who livest and reignest with the Father and the Holy Spirit, One God, world without end. *Amen.*

No. 53—*For a Pastor Entering upon the Duties of a Parish*

Almighty and Eternal God, Who dost call men to be pastors of Thy people and ministers of Thy grace: We thank Thee that Thou hast called Thy servant to minister to this congregation and to serve before Thee in Thy sanctuary; vouchsafe to him as he now begins his ministry in this place, the direction, aid and counsel of Thy Holy Spirit; that he may serve Thee with a pure heart and holy life; preach Thy Word according to Thy loving purpose in Christ Jesus; humbly and devoutly administer Thy sacraments; and be found in all things acceptable to Thee as a good and faithful steward; through Jesus Christ, Thy Son, our Lord. *Amen.*

Surprisingly perhaps, there was but one prayer by Reed under the heading Divine Worship.

No. 65—For Fruitful Hearing of the Word

Almighty and Everlasting God, Whose Word in the Holy Scriptures and in the ministrations of Thy house is implanted in our hearts, even as seed is sown in the ground: Grant us receptive minds, we pray Thee, good and honest hearts, free from selfishness and sin; so that by the quickening power of Thy Spirit we may become not hearers only, but doers of the Word; and, having the eyes of our understanding enlightened and the spirit of our mind renewed, be enabled to bring forth spiritual fruit in all goodness and righteousness and truth, proving what is acceptable unto Thee and serviceable to our fellowmen; through Jesus Christ, Thy Son, our Lord. *Amen.*

There were three prayers under the heading Education.

No. 117—For Pastors to Students

O Lord Jesus, Teacher and Saviour of men, Who didst say, Seek and ye shall find, knock and it shall be opened unto you: Grant Thine especial blessing to all pastors of students; give them that holiness of life which shall make them an example for others; enable them to enter into the problems of youth with sympathy and understanding, and to lead eager and inquiring minds beyond the things which are seen and temporal to the things which are unseen and eternal; Who livest and reignest with the Father and the Holy Ghost, One God, world without end. *Amen.*

No. 118—For Pastors to Students

O God of youth, and childhood, and of all men, to remember Whom in the growing years of life is to know the way to eternal joy: Grant that those who Thou hast sent to minister to the youth in institutions of learning may establish their lives upon the eternal foundations of righteousness, truth, and love, revealed in the holy life and teachings of Thy Son; to the end that they may be kept in communion with Thee in Thy Church; be enabled to live unto Thee in all pleasing, and be prepared for fruitful service to all men in their day and generation; through the Same, Thy Son, Jesus Christ our Lord. *Amen.*

No. 138—For Benefactors and the Grace of Giving

Almighty God, our Father, Who alone art the Author and Giver of all good gifts: Accept, we beseech Thee, our hearty thanks and praise for the labors and blessed memory of the founders of this institution, for its benefactors and for all who, by their gifts, their labors, or their prayers have befriended it. Raise up, we pray Thee, many sons and daughters in Thy Church to give freely of their substance according to its need for its growth and strengthening; give its teachers wisdom and all needful grace; and be pleased to bless it richly in all things temporal and spiritual as a nursery of faith, knowledge, and zeal for Thy cause among men; through our Lord and Saviour, Jesus Christ. *Amen.*

Under Gifts and Graces there was one prayer by Dr. Reed

No. 195—For Protection

O God, our heavenly Father, our Refuge and Strength, Who givest Thine angels charge over us to keep us in all thy ways: Grant us Thy almighty protection, we beseech Thee, in every danger that threatens the health and peace of our bodies; but especially, we pray Thee, do Thou protect our souls in all spiritual danger; deliver us from the power of our sins; in every temptation grant us Thine aid; make us strong to resist the evil and to choose the good, and save us by Thy grace; through Jesus Christ, Thy Son, our Lord. *Amen.*

Two prayers by Reed appear under the heading Our Daily Life.

No. 220—For Artisans

O Lord Jesus Christ, Who in Thine own city of Nazareth didst labor with Thy hands, and thus didst hallow all our toil: Look with Thy favor, we pray Thee, upon all craftsmen and workers whose daily occupations supply mankind with things needful for health, comfort and enjoyment. Grant strength to labor and joy in craftsmanship, so that ever striving to prove themselves workmen that need not to be ashamed, and doing all things as unto Thee, all who toil may be conscious of Thy comradeship and have Thy blessing upon all their handiwork; Who livest and reignest with the Father and the Holy Spirit, ever One God, world without end. *Amen.*

No. 221—For Those Engaged in Scientific Research

O God, the Father Almighty, Maker of heaven and earth and of all things visible and invisible; Whose glory the heavens declare; Whose handiwork the firmament showeth: Grant serious and reverent minds to all who study the marvels of Thy creation and seek to learn the processes of nature for the welfare of mankind; enable them to find in every increase of knowledge new manifestations of Thy divine power, wisdom and love; and as Thou hast created all material things, so do Thou create in us all clean hearts, attune with Thee, to the end that we may be led to know those things which, though not seen, are eternal; through Him Who is truth and life, even Jesus Christ, Thy Son, our Lord. *Amen.*

(This prayer continues in use in *For All the Saints* edited by Frederick J. Schumacher with Dorothy Zelenko, [Delhi, NY: ALPB, 1966] vol. IV, p. 257.)

Under the heading All Sorts and Conditions of Men, Dr. Reed, who was himself to suffer hearing loss, contributed one prayer, notable for its compassionate and hopeful tone.

No.266—For the Deaf

O Lord Jesus Christ, Whose compassion encompassed every infirmity of body and soul, and Who Thyself didst touch the ears of one that was deaf and opened them: Let Thy grace, we beseech Thee, rest upon all who suffer the loss of hearing; and grant that while they may not hear the sound of laughter or of music with the bodily ear, their hearts may ever know Thy loving voice, be joyous with Thy praise and be attuned to Thy Spirit; and find that harmony with Thyself which shall give them happiness in this life and joy in Thy presence for evermore; Who livest and reignest with the Father and the Holy Spirit, ever One God, world without end. *Amen.*

Finally, two prayers under the heading The City, the Nation, the World are from the hand and heart of Luther Reed.

No. 299—For the Nation and the President

Bless, we beseech Thee, merciful Lord, our country and our people. Give Thine especial aid and grace to the President of the United

States. Be his Counsellor and his Defense. Give him faith, wisdom, courage, health and patience to bear the burden of his office. Keep him in safety and grant that, relying upon Thee and seeking to do Thy will, he and his associates in government may enact wise laws and administer them justly, so that the welfare of our people may be assured and peace maintained at home and among the nations of the world; through Jesus Christ, Thy Son, our Lord. *Amen.*

No. 306—For the Armed Forces of the Nation

Almighty and Everlasting God, Whose Providence hath given unto us as a people this great land stored with treasure and around it hath cast like a mantle the sea: Bless, we pray Thee, the officers and men of our Army, our Navy, and our Air Forces, as they perform the duties of their calling: give them not only true love of country, but also love of Thee, and understanding of Thy love for all mankind; so that, relying upon Thine almighty aid, they may courageously defend our nation from every foe, promote righteousness, honor and unity among our people, in times of peace, and be a means of fostering mutual respect and understanding among the peoples of the world; through Jesus Christ, Thy Son, our Lord. *Amen.*

This prayer is included in the *Service Book and Hymnal* (1958) as no. 50 of Collects and Prayers, p. 225, and also in *For All the Saints* vol. IV, p. 893.

Two other prayers by Luther Reed are worthy of notice. The word edition of the *Common Service Book* (1919) supplemented the collection of Collects and Prayers in the music edition of the *Common Service Book* (1917, 1918) with seventeen Additional Collects under the headings For the Nation, For the President and Those in Authority, For the Church in Time of War, for the Army, For the Navy, For Those in Our Country's Service in Time of War, For Chaplains, For the Ministry of Mercy, For the Sick, Wounded and Captives, For the Bereaved, For Victory, For Peace, For the Discomfiture of the Enemies of the Nation, For the Maintenance of the Gospel, For the Parents and Friends of Men in the Service. Reed contributed two collects to this additional section. The first was

No. 88—For the Church in Time of War

O Lord Jesus Christ, Who didst establish Thy Church on earth, and didst command Thy disciples to be Thy witnesses among all nations: Grant unto Thy faithful people, amid the labors and distresses of this present time, boldness to confess Thy Name; enable them, by Thy Holy Spirit, to be among their fellowmen as those who serve, turning the hearts of men to Thee, uplifting the weak, comforting the sorrowing, and speaking peace to the desolate and afflicted; Thou Who livest and reignest with the Father and the Holy Ghost, ever One God, world without end. *Amen.*

This prayer was also included in the *Service Book and Hymnal* as no. 14 of the Collects and Prayers (p. 220).

Reed's second contribution was

No. 97—For Victory

O God, our Refuge and Strength, our very present Help in trouble: Protect and prosper, we beseech Thee, our beloved Country in this time of war; make of us, by Thy grace, a people worthy to be entrusted with victory; and so use, direct and bless our Army and Navy that they may be Thy chosen instruments in overcoming wrong and establishing liberty, truth and righteousness in the earth; through Jesus Christ, Thy Son, our Lord. *Amen.*

This prayer was also included in the *Service Book and Hymnal* as no. 54 of its Collects and Prayers (p. 226).

Endnotes

1 Paul Zeller Strodach (1876-1947), parish pastor and editor at the Lutheran Publication House in Philadelphia, was the author of *A Manual on Worship* (1930, rev. ed. 1946), *The Church Year* (1924), *The Road He Trod: A Spiritual Pilgrimage* (1932), *His Glorious Hour: A Passionale* (1932); he was the editor of vol. VI of the Philadelphia Edition of *Luther's Works,* Luther's Liturgical Writings (1932). His morning hymn "God of our life, all-glorious Lord" was included in the *Service Book and Hymnal* (no. 209) and *Lutheran Book of Worship* (no. 270); his Easter hymn "Now let the vault of heaven resound" appears in the *Service Book and Hymnal* (no. 103) and, slightly altered, in *Lutheran Book of Worship* (no. 143), *Lutheran Service Book* (no. 465), and *Evangelical Lutheran Worship* (no. 367).

2 George Rise Seltzer (1902-1974) contributed to *Collects and Prayers for Use in Church* (1935), served on liturgical commissions of the United Lutheran Church in America, but despite the urging of his students declined to write books, confident that his work would live on in his students. The author of this monograph is one of those students. His hymn for a church festival "Come, all ye people, come away" appeared in the *Service Book and Hymnal* (no. 249).

3 *For All the Saints* ed. Frederick J. Schumacher with Dorothy A. Zelenko, vol. II (Delhi, NY: ALPB, 1995), pp.318-319. Original publication in *Muhlenberg* [College] *Student Prayers* ed. John W. Doberstein (Allentown, Pennsylvania: Muhlenberg Christian Association, 1946), pp. 88-89; issued as *Prayers for Students* by the National Lutheran Council, 1947 and in a rev. ed. (Philadelphia: Muhlenberg Press, 1951). Dr. Doberstein was chaplain and professor of religion at Muhlenberg College 1943-1947 and after that Reed's colleague at the Philadelphia Seminary. In the introduction to his *Minister's Prayer Book* (1959) Doberstein calls Reed his "esteemed teacher and friend" (p. xxii).

4 *Collects and Prayers for Use in Church* authorized by the United Lutheran Church in America, prepared by the Common Service Book Committee (Philadelphia: Board of Publication of the United Lutheran Church in America, 1935), p. 123 no. 266—For the Deaf.

5 Dotterer after Charles Dotterer who married Luther Reed's maternal grandmother after her first husband had died.

6   *For All the Saints* vol. III, p. 959. Original publication in *Muhlenberg Student Prayers* ed. John W. Doberstein, (1946.)

7   *Memoirs of Henry Eyster Jacobs* ed. H[enry] E[yster] Horn, unpublished typescript, p. 356.

8   Thomas L. Edge reporting on his interviews with Luther Reed in November 1965 and February and July 1966 published as "Luther D. Reed," *Una Sancta* 23:4 (Christmass 1966), pp. 11-12. ["Christmass" is a spelling derived from "Christ mass" devised by Richard John Neuhaus, editor of *Una Sancta,* to distinguish the feast from the secular holiday.] Also in this fascinating interview Reed tells of his early study of liturgy with his fellow seminarian Thorkell Olaf Sigurdson, from Iceland, who had discovered in the seminary library a collection of Leonine, Gelasian, and Gregorian sacramentaries by Edmond Martene.

9   *The Life of Adolph Spaeth, D.D., LL.D.* edited by his wife [Harriet Reynolds Krauth Spaeth] (Philadelphia: General Council Publication House, 1916), pp.105-106.

10 James F. White, *A Brief History of Christian Worship* (Nashville: Abingdon, 1993), pp. 159-161.

11 *Memoirs of the Lutheran Liturgical Association* volumes I-II (Pittsburgh, 1907), pp. i-iv. I have in my possession Luther Reed's own copy of this volume, with his bookplate and his signature on the flyleaf.

12 For more on Harry Archer see Philip H. Pfatteicher, *Last on Grant: The History of the First English Lutheran Church in the City of Pittsburgh* (Minneapolis: Lutheran University Press, 2010), pp. 132, 142, 157, 160-163.

13 Philip H. Pfatteicher, *Last on Grant: The History of the First English Evangelical Lutheran Church in the City of Pittsburgh* (Minneapolis: Lutheran University Press, 2010), pp. 160-161.

14 Edge, pp.15-16. Endnote 5 of this essay (p. 25) gives the names of those in Germany and Scandinavia who gave Reed special hospitality and help.

15 *The Life of Adolph Spaeth,* pp. 379-380.

16 Quoted from the *Seminary Bulletin* in Theodore G. Tappert, *History of the Lutheran Theological Seminary at Philadelphia 1864-1964* (Philadelphia: Lutheran Theological Seminary, 1964), p. 111

17 *Common Service Book of the Lutheran Church* authorized by the United Lutheran Church in America (Philadelphia: Board of Publication of the United Lutheran Church in America, 1917, 1918), hymn no. 196.

18 Luther D. Reed, *Worship: A Study of Corporate Devotion* (Philadelphia: Muhlenberg Press, 1959), p. 153.

19 See Gordon W. Lathrop, "The Philadelphia Seminary and the Liturgy," *The Phil-adelphia Vision—Mt. Airy Tradition: Essays for the 125th Anniversary of the Lutheran Theological Seminary at Philadelphia* (Philadelphia, 1991), pp. 5-13.

20 My copy of the book was given to me by my aunt, Helen E. Pfatteicher, then on the staff of the Philadelphia Seminary Library, whose assistance, among others, is acknowledged in the Foreword of the book.

21 My copy bears the inscription, "Inscribed for Philip Henry Pfatteicher with appreciation of his interest in the Liturgy and Worship of the Church, and with very best wishes. Luther D. Reed Mt. Airy, Philadelphia, Nov. 23, 1960." When the *Lutheran Book of Worship* was published in 1978 Fortress Press asked Frank C. Senn and me to update Reed's *magnum opus.* We quickly saw that it was an impossible task. LBW was built on a rather different foundation than the restoration work that culminated in the *Service Book and Hymnal.* Each of us therefore worked on our portion of a new project, Pfatteicher publishing *Commentary on the Lutheran Book of Worship: Lutheran Liturgy in Its Ecumenical Context* (1990) and Senn publishing *Christian Liturgy: Catholic and Evangelical* (1997). The two books are parts of one whole.

22 Reed, *Worship,* p. xi.

23 Edgar S. Brown, Jr., "Luther Dotterer Reed: The Man," *Una Sancta* 23:4 (Christmass 1966), p. 133.

24 Edward Traill Horn III, "A 30th Anniversary Remembrance of the Publication of the Service Book and Hymnal," *The Bride of Christ* XII, 4 (St. Michael and All Angels, 1988), p. 12.

25 Theodore G. Tappert, *History of the Lutheran Theological Seminary at Philadelphia 1864-1964* (Philadelphia: Lutheran Theological Seminary, 1964), pp. 98-99.

26 Brown, p. 134.

27 The concluding lines of Reed's open letter.

28 "My history" is slightly misleading. The 1909 History of First Church Pittsburgh was in fact written by George Gongaware, then pastor of the parish, who in the introduction notes the significant assistance of Luther Reed.

29 Luther D. Reed, "At Eventide: Recollections and Reflections," unpublished typescript, 1959, p. 250.

30 Reed, "At Eventide," p. 250.

31 Reed, "At Eventide," pp. 62ff.

32 Horn, p. 12.

33 Edge, p. 9.

34 Luther D. Reed, "A Pan-Lutheran Liturgy and Hymnal," *Response* 7:4 (1966), p. 207.

35 Reported in Horn, p. 10.

36 Luther D. Reed, *The Spirit of the Philadelphia Seminary* (Mt. Airy, 1939), p. 17.

37 Edge, p. 22.

38 *Una Sancta* 23:4 (Christmass 1966), pp. 138-139. The note introducing this letter says Dr. Whitmer was a friend of Reed's "from seminary days." Whitmer was not a graduate of the Philadelphia Seminary, and the concluding remark in the excerpt suggests that he was in fact a medical doctor, a friend perhaps from college days.